Journey *into* Relationship

HAPPILY EVER AFTER
A TRUE STORY

—————— *by* ——————

Rita & Paul Christian

Tellwell Talent
www.tellwell.ca

ISBN
978-0-2288-9394-3 (Paperback)
978-0-2288-9395-0 (eBook)

Where is home?

The answer is as individual as we are. Some people have moved around all their lives and so 'home' changes with the geography.

We are not one of those people. We have lived in one place practically all of our lives. Not everyone has had the opportunity to stay put. We have been given a unique vantage point in our experience of home.

Home for us is Prospect Bay, Nova Scotia.

We are **Paul and Rita Christian.** As a **50th** wedding anniversary gift to each other, we have put our life story to paper.

We welcome friends and family to share our memories.

*If you don't know us, **<u>even better</u>**.*

Although the backdrop of your life will not be the same as ours, there are insights in our story that may help **you** celebrate your 50th wedding anniversary someday!!

Let's begin the journey.

CHAPTERS IN THE LIFE OF PAUL & RITA CHRISTIAN

CHAPTER 1

Paul's Mom & Dad

It will come as no surprise that Paul and I met and fell in love on Prospect Bay. That was 1967.

To backtrack a bit...here is how we each came to be in the same place at the same time.

Paul's great grandfather, grandfather and father were all lighthouse keepers off the shores of Prospect Village, on an island called Betty. Paul's dad, Milton, spent his adolescent years on Betty's island.

It is hard for this generation of kids to even imagine a world with no internet! Try wrapping your head around no other families, no kids to play with, and no motor on the boat that you used to go back and forth to the village of Prospect a few miles away. No need for an expensive gym membership when there were chores to do, supplies to carry, and boats to row in all weather conditions.

In every life, there are moments to cherish and moments to learn from.

Isolation provided both when Paul's dad was growing up.

One saving grace was his dog Tig(er). We are assuming he was a mixture of a Newfoundland dog and a lab. What we know for sure is that he was big, black and he loved to fish. Milton's mom would curse Tig's joy of diving into the water from heights on Betty's rugged shore and gleefully bringing home a fish, or two or three! He would leave these gifts on the rocks oblivious to the annoyance rotting fish would be to his family.

With only his dog for company, Milton looked forward to going to Prospect for social interaction. It was a welcome relief from the isolation of Betty's but also a disappointment. He saw that life could be just the same on the mainland. Booze would play a large role in his life. Good and bad.

In happy times, he met and married Muriel Duggan. She was born in Prospect, the last of 13 children! Milton, a.k.a. Tony, (everyone in Prospect had a nickname) was obviously a brave guy.

He and Muriel shared a long life together. They had four boys (Bruce, Patrick, Earl, Paul) and two girls (Eva and Marilyn). Paul is the last child they brought into this world.

Paul was born in Halifax on September 7, 1947.

Wages were scarce in Prospect. The federal pay cheque for tending a lighthouse that his dad and dad's dad had enjoyed was, even then, becoming a dead-end career choice, so off to the city of Halifax went the Christian brood. Milton went to work on the waterfront and the family lived in the city until Paul was about 7 years old.

Muriel, of course, still had family in Prospect and so, when transportation was available, they would visit… especially one of her sisters, Margaret. She too had left the village. After a time in Boston, Margaret's family settled on a property near the head of Prospect Bay.

The property was ample to accommodate two families and soon the sisters put their heads together. It was decided that Muriel and Milton would buy a parcel of land from Margaret.

1954 would mark the year that Paul called Prospect Bay home.

CHAPTER 2

Rita's Mom and Dad

My road to Prospect Bay.

Home for both of my parents was Halifax. There was a short stay in the Annapolis Valley where my dad, Warren Beswick, worked on the military base at Cornwallis. I was born in the nearby town of Annapolis Royal in 1952.

When I was 7, we moved to Spryfield, which was not annexed into the City of Halifax yet, but close enough that we could say we were "in town".

Growing up, summers for me meant going to "the beach" on Prospect Bay, opposite Purcell's Island.

My mom was Gladys Irene (Eveleigh) Beswick. My mom's dad (Ernest Eveleigh) bought the property back in the 30s (I think). Anyway, there are pictures of me as a toddler playing on the lawns outside the main house. The property was called, no surprise, Eveleigh's Beach.

The main house consisted of a sunroom facing the bay, with one bedroom off that. In the middle of the house was a huge dining room with a fireplace and a daybed, two more bedrooms off that room and toward the roadside was a large kitchen, back porch and bathroom. All of this was a second floor over the ground floor garage and storage which elevated the building to achieve beautiful views of Prospect Bay. Quite the cottage back then!!

The property also boasted 6 additional cottages which were often rented by the same families each summer, a canteen/cottage, boathouse, and a small common building we called The Hall. This building was multi-purpose but, most often, it was a place where about 50 people could eat picnic table style.

> My grandfather had an entrepreneurial spirit. He had left England as a very young man, stayed for a year or so in Newfoundland as a break in the journey to Nova Scotia. He became a successful businessman, a wheelwright. Mom grew up in an elegant house on Chebucto Road in Halifax. The third of six kids. She had two brothers and three sisters.

CHAPTER 3

Our Crossroads

Back to Eveleigh's Beach. The Hall came in handy for the dozens of company picnics that were held there during my childhood. Church groups, firemen, policemen, and big companies like Sears would rent the property to host a summer day of fun for their employees. There would be three legged races, lots of fun food, games, balloons, music and of course swimming and water toys.

When I was 15, one of the biggest picnics was held by the local Catholic church. Their chowder supper had grown in popularity and needed more space so, in 1967, they brought their picnic to Eveleigh's Beach.

I remember that picnic for a couple of reasons. One, they had a Ferris wheel, and two, Paul was there.

I had met Paul a few weeks earlier at a house party where all the local teens were gathered. We spent a lot of time talking that night and most days that followed. But it was at the Chowderama that Paul kissed me for the first time.

If you're doing the math, Paul was 19. My mother was not happy about our blooming romance. She couldn't think of any innocent reason for the attraction. I was 15.

Mom was not a light-hearted gal. Gladys was a woman out of sync with her generation. Rather than marriage and children, as a young woman, she wanted to work, to be independent. She was adventurous.

Culture pressure lives in all generations and she eventually broke under the strain. As a result, she carried her share of baggage and didn't spare feelings when there was a point to be made.

Imagine my surprise that, not many weeks into our "dating", she would be embroidering Paul's initials on his own pillowcase!

When school started and 'the beach" was closed for the season, I thought that was the end of the Paul and Rita story. It was a nice summer romance. I didn't envision a next step. Then the phone rang. Paul invited me on a date!!

He was taking me to supper and a movie.

My mom and dad gave us the thumbs up on the condition he brought me home by 10 p.m. They didn't realize that our mode of transportation would be by taxi. On our arrival home and the taxi had left the yard, Mom insisted that he sleep at our house so she wouldn't worry about him hitchhiking home.

Remember, my family was in Spryfield and Paul was in Prospect Bay, about 18 miles apart. He did not own a car yet. Even after transportation was not an issue, this trend continued until the house was sold in 1972.

As I teased above, by date number two, Paul had monogrammed pillowcases. Mom quickly transitioned from critic to cheerleader.

Paul was a charmer. If my mom was enamoured, what do you think my little heart was doing? I knew very early that he would be the love of my life. Bonus that he was great to look at, funny, smart, capable and confident. I was hooked.

Why did I love him from the beginning?

Simply, I was impressed.

Paul was all the adjectives above, plus he had integrity. He knew who he was.

I, on the other hand, was a work in progress.

I would eventually come into my own stage of life where I was blessed with a pleasing appearance but, back then, at 15 years old, I wore thick glasses, had acne and crooked teeth. I would never smile.

Paul saw "me" underneath all that confusion.

He held my hand through braces and literally helped me grow up. He guided me to make my own choices and helped me develop my own sense of who I was.

He always had vision. ☺

CHAPTER 4

Paul, The Early Years

Everyone has a story.

It's not your circumstance so much as what you are willing to do to change it that matters.

Paul's youth was not far off from his dad's. Isolated in a rural community, no kids around, drunk father, poor, no privacy or empathy.

On the positive side, he had freedom to adventure on his own, go into the woods, find his own way, make choices. Paul grew to trust his own rationale and his own abilities.

He had lots of chores at an early age... things like replenishing the firewood, fixing things, loading the bottles of oil for the KeMacstove and going to work (for Sears) at 14 to help keep food on the table. This taught Paul responsibility.

People with similar backgrounds often become bitter.

Because God blessed him with a happy heart, a solid, caring, contributing man emerged. In his time alone, he created his own Code, behaviours to live by. He had expectations of himself. For example, his handshake meant something to him.

A few other challenges. Paul's dad was in his 50s when he was born. His siblings were already married with kids. Marilyn was the exception. She is 7 years his senior. Marnie lived at home, but much of her time would be spent at her sister's in the city.

No surprise, Paul often felt like a stranger in his own home.

CHAPTER 5

Paul & Prospect Bay Growing Up Together

Part of what we hope to do in writing down our memories is to paint a picture of the physical changes on Prospect Bay over 6 or 7 decades.

In the mid 1950's, the road to Prospect was unpaved. There was only a scattering of houses along the road between White's Lake and Prospect. Aunt Margaret's was the first property from the turn off and Paul's house was, as I explained, next door.

The original lot stretched from the road to the shore of Prospect Bay. When Milton and Muriel chose where the house would be, they decided as close to the water as possible.

The house foundation was bulldozed. Excavators were not an option back then. Materials were also at a premium, so people were innovative and helped each other. A nephew, Billy Hammond, had a coal business. That's how the foundation of the house came to be set on a bed of coke. (burnt coal). The foundation of cinder block has never shifted or leaked.

How do we know? That's where Paul and I live, that's our home.

In placing the house close to the water, they knew that a retaining wall would be needed. Son, Bruce, worked at CN Railway and had access to railroad ties. A combination of ties, rock and timber made a 64' wharf and a 4' (or so) wall at the highwater mark. This would be backfilled over the years as money and opportunity allowed.

Paul learned to swim here. The water was full of things little boys like to catch. Hermit crabs, starfish, a variety of jellyfish including those that are about the size of a silver dollar and about the same colour. It is home to a variety of seagulls and ducks. Eagles and geese are common. Mink and otters come and go. Even the occasional seal.

Paul and sister Marnie (Marilyn) became adept at spearing eels, a favourite food of their parents. An eel or two back then would be enough to provide a meal. Some would be so large that it was heavy and awkward to get them in the boat.

You might have guessed that in order to have eels, you have to have eelgrass. Unlike today, the whole head of the bay was so full of grass that it was difficult, if not impossible, to row at low tide. The work to widen and eventually pave the Prospect Road contributed to changing the ecosystem in this part of the bay. Gravel and silt don't mix well with grass.

When Paul was a boy, a variety of fish were available just off the property wharf.

Paul playing near the wharf

Every species seemed to have a season and they would come in schools. Pollock, flatfish, frostfish, sea trout, mackerel and the occasional tommy cod. There were smelt brooks close by and lots of berries on the islands (especially Purcel's) and cranberries in the bog across the road.

Clams, periwinkles and mussels were at the doorstep which were largely used for bait. He remembers them all being much larger than the ones we see today.

Opposite the property was a small island which was a perfect weather break. (We will come back to this later in the story). Looking out the window, the head of Prospect Bay would be to the left where the river flowed in from White's Lake. Across the bay and to the right looking south, there was nothing. No houses, no lights, just a lot of trees.

The Prospect uncles were primarily deep-water fishermen. They were generous with feeds of the larger fish varieties like cod, halibut and, of course, lobster. The Christian house became a common stop over for trips between Prospect and Halifax.

Paul spent his days either on the water or across the road in the woods, primarily in the wedge of land that is between Shad Bay and Prospect Road. A variety of food was not abundant at home, so Paul was encouraged to hunt. It was a happy day when he brought home rabbits, partridge or pheasants. He did this all his young years.

(This is just a glimpse of the huge changes we have seen and experienced in our lifetime. From unpaved roads, hunting and fishing at the doorstep to quantum computing!!)

The wharf eventually succumbed to winter ice and storms.

Over the years the property was augmented by copious wheelbarrow loads from work sights when the road was rebuilt. Pits were developed along the route to house a steam shovel (powered by coal) and a rock crusher. One such site was close by so Paul helped his dad move spent material from the pit back home to level off the property. This was long before ordering a load of gravel to be delivered was even dreamed of, let alone affordable.

The house was built in stages, one storey at a time. Before the second floor was tackled, Bruce married. Although Paul was too young to understand the complexities of the manoeuvring that occurred, the result was Bruce took over the house. Paul's mom and dad began anew, with depleted resources, to build a much smaller one level, two-bedroom home, next door.

Winters would be long and hard. Time was filled with chores and doing kid things like jumping ice flows in the bay. Paul spent a lot of time with his dog. Like his dad, a saving grace in his early life was a Belgian shepherd named Scamp. I got to know her, but she died shortly after Paul and I met. It still brings tears to his eyes to remember her.

It wasn't all sad. Paul's mom, Muriel, tried her best to lighten the mood. She was a tremendous cook. The kind that could make something out of nothing. She was happy to feed whoever showed up.

There was always fresh homemade bread. She loved to bake and have little surprises for Paul after school. St. Patrick's Day called for green milk and cookies.

Although I was relatively young when we started dating, our conversations were always adult in nature. Paul was the kind of guy who did not enjoy silliness. (Remember he had a Code.) For example, throwing people in pools or practical jokes would make him angry and his friends learned very quickly that they risked a quick payback if they tried.

Both of our home lives had their ups and down. I touched on Paul's situation. Their home was tiny. Paul shared a room with his father and Marilyn with her mom. Unconventional but the better alternative from his parent's point of view. Beside the two bedrooms, there was a small living room, smaller kitchen and a bathroom.

When the house was built, it was among the first in the area to have indoor plumbing. (The area was primarily seasonal cottages.) That was the *only* luxury.

Growing up, there would be no quiet spaces to read or study.

The 'old man' would dictate the tone in the household. He was either drunk or mad that he wasn't. Tony was not a bad man. He was a frustrated one.

In my opinion, he felt angry that he couldn'tprovide better. He worked hard. He had a good head on his shoulders but could never pull himself, or his family, into a better life. At least that was the excuse I landed on.

CHAPTER 6

Rita Growing Up

My physical surroundings were more comfortable. Our home was modest but met all our needs.

I had one sibling. My sister, Carol, was 9 years old when I came along. She was not happy to share our parent's attention. We never really bonded. Carol was working, engaged and out of the house by the time I was 10 or 11. Bonus for me! That meant I had the bedroom all to myself with her vacated twin bed ready for overnight guests. Sweet.

My parent's bedroom and mine were upstairs in our 1½ story house. Downstairs there was a front room, kitchen, bathroom and den with a pull-down coach. Paul finally had a room to himself!

As you now know, my mom's family had Eveleigh's beach. My grandfather, Ernest, left this world when I was about 3. The ownership of the beach shifted to the two Eveleigh sons, Cecil and Fred. My grandfather was not from a time where girls were seen as capable or worthy. This was a sore spot for my Mom all her life.

Like I mentioned earlier, she wanted to be a career person. Instead, she was forced by her father to manage the family home (her mom, Vida, was always ill).

To accomplish getting Gladys to do his bidding, Ernest went to her employer (Moir's Chocolates) and pressured them to let her go. Trapped, she eventfully fell in line with the acceptable trends of her day which meant doing what she was told and eventually marriage and children. She was a reluctant wife and mother. She was dutiful but never truly joyful in those roles.

Don't get me wrong. She loved us. It just wasn't her dream job. On his deathbed, her dad told her: "You are the only Eveleigh in the bunch". She cherished that sentiment for the rest of her life.

In my late teens, mom had a meltdown. One day I came home from work to learn that they had sold my bedroom furniture. Then they casually dropped the bomb that they were selling the house and moving to a ***one-bedroom*** apartment.

I was devastated. I was about to be homeless.

For the best part of our engagement year, I slept on a coach in mom's apartment, (they actually moved again because she wasn't comfortable with the first choice) or at my sister's or, more often than not, opposite Milton's lazy boy chair at Paul's house with only a blanket draped chair for privacy.

It was Paul's steady hand on my shoulder that kept me from my own spiral into depression.

It wasn't always like that. I had a great childhood. Both mom and dad tried hard to give us the best life possible. I never lacked for anything important. I had a nice home plus I was blessed to be able to spend a lot of time on Prospect Bay.

Our family also did fun things like Sunday drives for ice cream. We went camping. We took trips to visit Dad's extended family and often shared time with aunts and cousins. Paul even got to join us on one trip to Cape Breton. We all had a good time.

Dad took great pride in making Christmas cakes and Halloween taffy apples. Mom loved Christmas mornings… she couldn't make herself wait beyond 5 a.m. She would make enough noise to make sure everyone was up and ready to open presents.

Looking back, mental health issues were common in her family. Perhaps it was heredity. No one has confirmed that.

Her mom had displayed an inability to cope with normal family responsibilities. Mom lost a brother to suicide when I was in my teens, just prior to meeting Paul. A niece was diagnosed bipolar, but it seemed more severe.

Keeping with this trend, my mom came to a point where she was not able to deal calmly with realities. Maybe that is why I lean toward being the opposite - always dealing with stuff head on.

Perhaps it's an unconscious defence mechanism. 😃

CHAPTER 7

The Foundation Years

So, you see, our families gave Paul and I a fairly rich range of subjects for our conversations. Not surprising, given the chaos in our home lives, we loved being together. As time passed, things that used to fill our individual time started to fade into the background as we both **made choices to make each other the priority.**

We mostly preferred to be by ourselves. We were exploring new ground.

Neither Paul nor I came from a background where emotions were expressed. It was uncommon to get a hug or kiss from our families.

I craved a relationship that was rich in physical touching. In the beginning, Paul would pull away if I sat beside him too closely or reached for his hand. Because it made me happy, he relented. We were in love. It wasn't a huge problem. Before too long, he was looking forward to it as much as I.

This expression of love is part of our life, even today. Being vulnerable is a choice.

It takes courage to allow yourself to trust and to feel deeply.

Paul and I also enjoyed time with a variety of groups that satisfied our social urges. We have spent time with very nice people, but eventually interests changed and those relationships stopped growing.

Often, for us, it was others who went on to have children. It was our choice not to conceive a child for reasons we will get into later.

There is a time and season for everything.

It was important for us to enjoy the present and not get too far ahead of ourselves.

We tried not to waste a lot of time looking back or too far ahead.

Paul and I have always tried to reach a little beyond where we were. We wanted to be better people. Not that we didn't like who we were. It was a simple challenge that we both enjoyed.

Fun example.

We created a game where we put a word we didn't use much on a card with the pronunciation and meaning on the other side. It was a way to expand our vocabulary.

We would play the game while driving to work. It helped us recognize the habits we wanted to break like saying "you know" as part of every sentence and relying on profanity when we were frustrated.

We also made a point to sharpen our social graces - things like table etiquette. We wanted to be confident no matter what environment we found ourselves in. Sophistication was not part of either of our backgrounds. It had to be learned.

We never got tired of talking together.

Life is not easy for anyone. It was fun for Paul and I to **try to flatten the curve ahead of any crisis**. We tried to avoid the things that could break a relationship.

Nobody we have met to date has shared this approach.

Sooner or later, we seem to wear people out. Not everyone likes to chat about life, religion or politics.

Imagine that!!

I say this tongue in cheek to make fun of ourselves. We do have moments of seriousness, but life was always fun and as light-hearted as we could manage.

We laughed a lot.

Chapter 8

We Are Engaged!

Did I mention that Paul is a very romantic man? Well, he is.

The rings he chose were lovely. Two identical engraved bands with a tasteful solitaire diamond on one. I looked forward to having them both on my finger. Starry skies over a private stretch of Prospect Bay shoreline was the backdrop to his proposal. It was magical.

We decided on a date (May 26, 1973) giving ourselves roughly a year to prepare. It was such a wonderful time of learning and understanding each other.

We would make up **"what if" questions** and then go back and forth until we came to common ground.

Even though we had already had five years of conversations, we delved even deeper to uncover what we valued, what we hoped for, *who* was important, *what* was important, *where* we wanted to live, *how* we wanted to live and on and on.

Part of the fun was "**I don't want**" lists.

Those were easy to articulate, and they helped us map a direction. They provided a solid foundation to build on.

Communication is the foundation for all relationships.

Marriage, friendships and spiritual connection all require a lifetime of sharing your innermost feelings and understanding.

Feelings and understanding are not cemented in time. They grow and change.

As long as we draw breath, we are created by God to travel a life journey of building and maintaining relationships, both with each other and with Him.

Hence the title of this book.

CHAPTER 9

Things to Consider

Here is a glimpse into some of the topics Paul and I explored. Some will seem trivial (even eye rolling) but, believe us, we short circuited countless potential hurts based on these talks.

Discussion was just that, a fun banter. With no real-time catalyst to set off an explosion, it became a fun conversation.

<u>Money</u>

Should we maintain individual bank accounts, or do we operate with one? Are we open with what we earn or do we divide up our joint cost of living responsibilities and each take on those payments. Does any money leftover stay in a personal account, or do we pool everything? Spendthrift or miser?

<u>What atmosphere</u> <u>did we want to live in</u>?

Some people like natural wood, some like simple white walls. Some want magazine quality furnishings. Some people prefer cozy to elegant. We had to figure out what our home would feel like. Do we want things to be neat or is a little clutter part of the charm?

We have all visited places where the connection between the people and the home (whether it be apartment or house) seems off. For instance, lots of pink or floral prints in places where one person lives in denim and work boots. Obviously one person made the decisions and the other didn't communicate their preferences. We did not want to be them.

Early birds or night hawks?

Laugh all you want, but we have witnessed this one factor to be a game changer.

Children? If yes, when? How many? Strict or lenient?

God? Factor or not?

If yes, will faith be central, a sidebar or put off for down the road, if ever? Sacramental or legal? How did we view our marriage vows?

Time and Attention?

Time with each other versus time with others? What are our priorities?

Alcohol and/or Drugs?

What part if any will they play in our life. If yes, what would be acceptable parameters?

Attitude toward the words "work" and "play"

If need be, could we make chores or responsibilities as much fun as playing a sport or other recreational activity?

Physical Expectations Some things are out of our control but, within reason, what would be a turn off?

Privacy Expectations Do we open a closed door (especially the bathroom) without knocking? If a letter is in one person's name, is that fair game for the other to open? Are wallets or purses private? Do we share passwords, email, or conversations with friends and family members? Do we keep secrets from each other?

Rules for Arguing We knew that there would be times that we would do or say things that would not sit well with the other person. Paul is the type that shuts down and walks away. I am a let's-deal-with-it-now-type.

Obviously, something had to give. Our middle road was to set a time limit on the cold shoulder treatment. We are talking hours, not days. We force ourselves not to ignore whatever set us off but to try to replay the event and figure out what parts wereJour hurtful.

I cry easily. Paul saw that as a disadvantage to his argument because he hates to see me cry. I was able to disarm him which was unfair, so I had to learn to talk rationally and be able to put to words what I was feeling. He had to do the same. It was not easy, but we knew it was better than the alternative where nasty things can be said in anger.

Say you are sorry all you want… those angry words stay in your head. If we can leave you with any pearls of wisdom, this is an important one. Every couple is different. Figure out what would work for you and be true to the rules you decide on.

Do everything you can to avoid hurting each other.

These conversations were not drudgery. We didn't approach it like a list of rules or opportunity to one-up the other. Our attitude was always on the positive side…the more we could come to common ground, the closer we were to each other. It was, and still is, a way of growing together.

It was never a competition or a battle of wills.

Attitude is key to good communication. We always expected that the other had the best intentions. Our promise to each other was - *You look after me, I look after you.* That way, there was no room, or need, to be selfish. Love is like that.

Highlights and lowlights of our engagement year.

I touched on my mother's meltdown and my homelessness earlier which, of course, is a huge lowlight for that year. She took no joy in shopping or making choices for the upcoming wedding. It was just another thing that she found difficult to deal with.

But an equally huge highlight of our engagement year was spending time with Fr. Greg Hennan. In answer to one of the questions we had explored about God and faith, we had come to a decision.

Thanks to both sets of parents, Jesus Christ was not a stranger. We were far from mature in matters of faith, but we knew the basic Gospel message. We knew we were adopted children of God the Father. We understood that He made us each a unique creation. Out of love for us, His son Jesus died on the cross to bear the consequence of our sin.

Yes, God was important to each of us. Yes, we wanted God in our life. But there was a dilemma.

Paul was raised Catholic and me Anglican. What church would we go to? Paul didn't want to push *his* way and I was equally pliable. So to be fair, we decided to shop for a church. We looked up different services from a variety of denominations and each week we would go to a different service.

It didn't take long to realize that we wanted a **sacramental marriage**. To us that meant that we would invite God to be a part of our union.

We had learned that the Eucharistic celebration was virtually word for word the same in each of our traditions and so, because the faith of Paul's family was more entrenched than mine, I volunteered to attend RCIA (Rite of Catholic Initiation for Adults). Enter Fr. Greg Heenan who was Paul's sister Eva's parish priest.

Fr. Greg was a very patient guy. Folded arms over my chest were the first indication that I was not about to drink all the Kool Aid, but I was open to listen. Every Tuesday evening over the fall and winter of 1972/73, he met with both Paul and I for lively discussions. No questions were too trivial, and I had a ton of them! Tuesday became a time that all three of us looked forward to.

I was confirmed into the Catholic faith by the Bishop during a province-wide Jubilee Year celebration (only every 50 years), on Saint Mary's field in Halifax with dozens of other newbies. It was a grand initiation celebration; it was Easter Sunday AND it was my 21st birthday!

We were married by Fr. Greg a month later. Such a blessing! By this time, we had grown to love each other making our wedding Mass very intimate. Paul, me, God and Fr. Greg.

We were off to a great start! Many years later, we would visit Fr. Greg in his retirement, shortly before his death, to have him pray a blessing over new wedding bands - the old ones were worn out!

The RCIA program helped us grow in our faith. It also focused us on our upcoming married life and not so much on planning a wedding.

We kept the most important things, the most important things.

CHAPTER 10

The First 10 Years

After a very short honeymoon to Maine, Paul and I settled into the rhythm of living together.

We rented the middle flat in a three story walk up on Stanford Street in Halifax. 'Flat' meaning that we occupied the whole floor! We had a front and back door, porch, large kitchen with a washing machine, bedroom, a second bedroom that we used as a TV room, bathroom and a front room that we could not furnish just yet, so we set up a pool table. Oh, to be young and silly!

That would be *home* for 2 ½ years. The best part for me was that, after being a nomad for about a year, everything I owned was finally in one place. Yeah.

Learning to live together was an exercise in being considerate. We both tried to be conscious of doing things that would be helpful, or, at least, not annoying for the other.

I didn't overpower the bathroom vanity with makeup or insist on "girly" things in the house. Paul always left the sink clean after he shaved. He would hang towels straight. He always put dirt clothes in the hamper. In short, we learned to do little things that added to the enjoyment of life together and avoided doing things that would be an irritant.

One of the reasons that we came back from Maine early was that Paul was still a team member in a softball league. Duty called.

With no pressure from me (ardent scorekeeper), Paul decided to "retire" from playing ball. He wanted to devote all his time to me / us.

It may seem odd to some readers that we would limit our time with social groups. Perhaps God had a plan from the beginning.

I was in my first full time job as a secretary to three guys. Paul was a pipefitter apprentice when we met. Although his future was bright, he knew that it was not a lifestyle that he would enjoy long term.

He was a trained draftsman and so he left the higher construction salary to work with an architectural firm. Again, he did well.

It didn't take long before he transitioned to the City of Halifax planning group. He would prepare information regarding pending developments for Council and would review and make recommendations on building permits. That was where he was working when we married. We still have wedding gifts from the staff that we use daily.

"Funny" story. A developer was pressuring Paul to approve a building permit, but it did not meet the criteria so, Paul was recommending that the project be declined.

Under the table, he was offered a colour TV delivered to our apartment. No need for us to be home - they *knew* where we lived!! Paul, of course, would not take a bribe so the developer got very angry and threatened that he had other building sites where "people" could disappear without a trace. Paul joked about the perks of the job. I didn't find it funny.

With Marilyn, Paul and I at work during the day, it was considered a prudent choice to have a dog that would be both company for Paul's mom and dad and a deterrent to any unwanted company.

We got Shannon, a black Labrador Retriever, from a litter raised by people I worked with. They had promised us a male and, as it happened, Shannon was the only boy in the bunch. They were true to their word. He came to jointly live with Paul and I and his mom and dad.

In 1975, we moved to a house in Bayside (just past Prospect Bay). A friend of Marilyn's owned it, but she was moving to Ontario. We were asked to consider moving in.

It was a lovely house on the water, but it was never one that felt like our home. Home was Prospect Bay, and we felt the pull every time we drove by that exit.

As a reminder, Bruce had taken over the first attempt at building next door to Aunt Margaret. He raised his family in this house.

Towards his retirement from CNR, he was offered a position in Bridgewater, N.S. Bruce had been a hands-on guy all his working life. Always doing the hard jobs himself to spare sending someone else. He was known for his dedication and ability, especially when there was a wreck. So, the job in Bridgewater was sort of a reward, an easier position.

The bad news was that he had to move from Prospect Bay where he had family on both sides. They decided to go, but instead of selling their home, they rented it to a work colleague for a year to give themselves the ability to reconsider.

Tenants are seldom a happy experience. Bruce decided to sell, and Paul and I had the first option. Believe it or not, it was not an easy decision. Paul and I both loved Prospect Bay. This is where we met and where we spent a good portion of our childhoods. Prospect Bay is where we were meant to be.

The BUT was a couple of things. First, we would be living next door to his sister, mom and dad on one side and Ethel, Margaret's daughter, on the other. Sounds fine? There were more things on the negative side for me.

Could we make this place our own? Would the family always refer to Bruce's place? Bruce and his dad were drinking buddies. There was a dynamic there that Paul was not a part of.

Paul was younger, he lived in a world they didn't understand. They could not even tell you what he did for a living. Secondly, the interest rate on the existing mortgage was 23%. The buyer had to agree to assume the mortgage and there was 3 or 4 years left on the term. That was a lot of money for us.

So, we went out in the boat, sat on Strawberry Island and debated what we should do. You know the answer already. It would put us under a financial strain, but we went for it.

Before the ink was dry on the Bill of Sale, Paul gutted the inside of the house. I nearly died. We didn't own it yet for crying out loud. We moved in December 1977 but had to leave plywood up to the bedroom window so we could get the moulded shower in the house. That didn't come until February!

We didn't have money, but we had energy, a bit of talent and determination. Bit by bit, year after year, this property has changed and improved. We are proud of what we have accomplished.

We are most proud of the teamwork that it took.

The best way to build a solid relationship? - simply do things together.

For us it was things like working on the house or property. Exercise. Our volunteer works. Social activities. Everything was done together.

With our backgrounds, it was understandable that we would be nesters - our home is a refuge, not just a house. A solid base was essential to our mental health.

Live the life <u>you</u> have chosen - ***together***.

If you find yourself dividing up the jobs, then the caution flag should go off in your head. Stay on the same path, share everything.

Every decision we made was based on how well it met those needs. If a job required us to work alternate hours. We refused. If we had to drive in different directions, in different cars, we refused. We both do housework. We both do yard work. We both pay bills. We have the same friends. Get the picture?

Please don't go off the deep end here. Of course, you must encourage each other to grow and develop as individuals, but only if that strengthens the whole.

Again: *I look after you, you look after me.*

Never put yourself first.

That's another pearl of wisdom 50 years of marriage can offer.

In marriage there is only one life, not two.

Like it or not, God created marriage.

To experience its full potential, it must include Him.

We, as a modern society, like to believe WE are in control. We are not.

If you are adamant that your world will remain the same after you marry and the only change you are willing to make is your address, then save yourself the trouble. You are on a fool's errand.

We are not suggesting that all marriages will fail without God.

What we do believe is that there will be no true joy in those unions.

CHAPTER 11

Thoughts on Raising a Family

Some people know very early in life that they want to have a family.

Even with the complications of the families Paul and I were born into, the possibility of having children was something we talked about a lot.

Most of our friends made that decision early in their marriage. We witnessed their approach and it seemed to us that parenting quickly became a balancing act of dealing with the challenges that each day presented but there didn't seem to be an end goal in mind.

In our talks, Paul and I tried to envision our adult children and asked ourselves what qualities we would hope they had. We came up with a list of adjectives that looked something like this: Confident, loyal, loving, truthful, kind, generous, grateful, helpful, considerate, prayerful . . . the list went on.

Note the list did NOT contain doctor, lawyer, rich, powerful, etc.

Then the question shifted to how to nurture a child to become that adult.

Obviously, there are no clear-cut answers, but it made for fun conversations.

One of things that we tossed around was having a growth chart.

Most parents took pleasure in measuring their kid's physical growth and marking that progress on a door frame.

What if, we thought, side by side with a growth chart, was a fun list of goals for the child to achieve. The chart would be a constant in the household. They would grow up seeing the words beside little steps that were achievable and age appropriate for them to work towards.

We felt it important that, even from a very young age, nurturing a sense of accomplishment was important.

Parents always want the best for their children. They give them life experiences, do fun things for them and provide for their physical needs.

Although the intention is there, it is often not understood by the child the "why" behind the rules that are presented to them.

Paul grew up in a household of adults that were focused on day-to-day things that had to be done to survive. There were moments of calm, but the overlying atmosphere was chaos, fuelled by booze. Every male in the family drank. Everyone argued. As long as he wasn't underfoot, and not causing any problems, he had no guidance.

My parents were dealing with less critical but similar stresses. The common thread was the constant bickering. If the sky was blue, the other would say it was going to rain. It all seemed to be ridiculous, tedious, senseless. When I asked questions, the answer was always "because I said so." I hated not understanding the point.

Our own childhood experiences helped us picture a better approach.

We knew that a fundamental goal was to teach a child, first and foremost, that they were a child of God. Perfect in their imperfections. (We all have them.) They were special.

Guidance is given out of love rather than being a deterrent.

These hypothetical parenting how-to's lasted for years.

In the meantime, we witnessed other families mature and many of the children were now in their teens. It was a sad observation that most were not happy stories.

The exceptions always had a commonality. The parents had been intentional, and they took the time with their children to nurture their formation.

It seemed to Paul and I that the joy for a lot of people in having a child leaned toward selfish and perhaps that contributed to the less than hoped for results.

We know that sounds harsh and we don't want to paint with a broad brush. It is never a conscious approach for anyone. Something in all our psyches needs to love and be loved.

A baby brings the parent joy. One friend described their baby as "the ultimate toy." They explained "You get to dress them up, show them off, it's an excuse to dream".

The dreams they had for their child seemed to fill the holes that were missing in their own childhood. They were looking forward to being part of the child's journey.

The misconception seemed to be that the child was self-directed. They were smarter than their parents. From our vantagepoint, this philosophy was misguided.

Our lesson learned. Parenting is primarily leading by example. If you are a parent, you are expected to teach.

We took the decision to parent very seriously. Having elderly parents ourselves made it an even harder choice. Time would tell.

CHAPTER 12

Brian, Part One

A few months after our wedding, Paul was asked to do the orientation for a new hire from Ontario. His name was Brian, and he would fill a new position entitled Urban Planner. Back then, this was a newly minted degree and graduates were in demand across the country. Brian and Paul hit it off immediately. Me, not so much.

Brian had recently returned from 8 months backpacking throughout Europe, Greece, Afghanistan, India and a bunch of other places I don't recall. Suffice to say, Paul was very taken with his tales of adventure. They were polar opposites and so I guess it was reasonable that they bonded.

Brian and I were polite to each other, but we were NOT friends. In fact, he viewed me as a mistake and I saw him as a threat to my husband's satisfaction with his life choices.

For example, he invited Paul to join him on his next adventure overseas and Paul gave it serious consideration. He even got his shots and was an inch away from buying a plane ticket. It was a pivotal moment in our relationship.

I told Paul that if this was something he needed to experience, he had my blessing to go. We both knew it would be life changing. He would see and experience things that I would not share. At the same time, I may not be the same on his return.

I sat my parents down and told them of the pending trip and that I would not tolerate any interference or judgment. There was a poster that I had seen in a store and it said, "if you love something, let it go". I had made up my mind that the decision was Paul's to make, I was not standing in the way.

As you will remember, our marriage is a sacrament. There are three of us in this union. God played his part.

Out of the blue, Paul was offered a new and better job with the Province of Nova Scotia. The start date conflicted with his travel plans. He decided to stay. We didn't acknowledge the spiritual aspects at the time, but looking back, God knew what was best for us. He kept us together and on the same path. There has never been a regret on either side.

Although Brian and Paul didn't go to Europe together, they treasured their friendship.

Halifax had been a steppingstone in Brian's career. He stayed about a year then was off to other positions in Ontario, finally settling in Edmonton where he was very successful.

Paul and he would find ways of going to the same conferences and Paul made numerous trips west where they would share hiking adventures. Most years, one of them would travel to the other. Paul got to experience the Rockies a half dozen times. Brian would often come to Prospect Bay for his summer vacations.

Brian eventually married. They met when both were Commonwealth students in London. Home for Heather was South Africa. Their romance was one suitable for a novel, but it did not have the foundation under it to survive. Divorce is hard, even if it is what you thought you wanted.

When the separation dust was settling, Brian again came to spend time with us during the summer. He arrived by motorcycle, driving with very little rest, all the way from Edmonton. As it happened, I was between jobs. Another God nod?

Brian and I finally got to appreciate each other. Again, it was time together that made the difference.

We had fun drives on the bike all over the province and we would race to get to the house before Paul. More than once, we passed Paul on his drive home after work. We were just a blur going by.

For the record, I am not condoning reckless driving here. Time on a motorcycle leaves an impression. I loved it. Paul and I had each bought bikes in Year 2 of our marriage when we were living in Bayside.

Our safety course required driving up and down a teeter totter, along 20 feet of ropes to simulate gravel and actually laying down a bike in case of emergency.

This was another foundation that ensured that we survived the experience.

CHAPTER 13

Spiritual Journey

We have shared that God was part of our discussions during our engagement year. Those good intentions were short lived.

Church was a struggle for us. We strongly disliked the environment and were very good at criticizing everything from the priest (no, not our Fr. Hennan), to the music, to the service itself.

So, like most young couples, we excused ourselves from our spiritual promises and instead decided that we would appreciate God from afar, preferably from the golf course or hiking trail or anywhere we wanted to be, except in church.

After all, we were busy. We had parents to look after. Pets. Snowmobiles to ride. Sports to play. House to rebuild. Places to visit. The first trip was to Barbados! Who had time for church?

God did not let us ignore him for very long.

In 1979, we participated in a christian retreat called Cursillo. It was a wonderful experience.

I will share one God moment that was especially for me. On paper I was a Catholic, but I was a stranger to the nuances of the Mass. It was never fully explained to me the whys behind the gestures or the meanings behind the words. There was a tendency back then for people to view anyone who was not born into the faith as an interloper. Priests were set apart. Nothing felt inviting.

Cursillo changed that for me when Fr. Phil sat with the group on the floor of the Mother House at Mount Saint Vincent University, played his guitar, and led us in the most beautiful, intimate celebration of the Mass that I had ever shared. I heard and understood in my heart aspects of that Eucharistic thanksgiving that I relive at every Mass since.

With the flame of love of God reignited, Paul and I spent the next 10 years working within that movement. We worked with Challengers (under 15 year olds), Antioch (16-21 year olds) and the adults in Cursillo. It was a privilege to explore faith with all the people we met during that period. Those shared experiences formed a bound that has lasted throughout our life. De Calores!

Community church seemed to be an obvious thing to add to the mix. We gave it a good try. We served on the Parish Council, led a youth group, and participated in the parish in any way we were asked. Gosh, we loved those kids. Our house was full all the time. Later in life, it was not unusual for us to get a hug in the grocery store from an adult who was once one of "our" kids.

Still, the Sunday church environment was not the family feel that we craved from our faith community. People fighting over where to sit. People doing the same things for years and years and never offering to train someone to do the same. We saw it. We didn't like it. Our immaturity skewed our vision. The focus was on what **we** needed and not so much on what we should offer to change it.

There is an ebb and flow to all things. Cursillo attracted fewer participants and so, for us, it came to an end. So did our youth group.

"Our seat" in the pew was up for grabs. No, God did not let us go. We thought we were finished. Time for a break.

Then the phone rang. "Hi", said Fr. Ron. "I need your help". "I am putting together the Marriage Preparation Course for the Diocese and I want you two to lead it". "But we aren't going to church" we confessed. "We don't have children." "We don't have the skills to pull it off". Our excuses fell on deaf ears. Fr. Ron has an easy way about him and one of his charisms is that he is very persuasive. So, guess what we did for the next 5 years?

Then we burned out. We sank back into a non-participant role and stayed there a long time.

CHAPTER 14

Glimpse of Life Then

The following years, with our faith journey on hold, were full of fun things that balanced out the work and serious side of life.

Shortly after they met, Paul and Brian started to run which was not a common pursuit back then. In time, being a team player, I did as well. Paul and I also joined the YMCA, which led to meeting a thriving group of active people for 7 a.m. classes led by Suzanne.

We went to lots of get togethers, like the mid-winter Margarita Party, where we all dressed in festive clothing. The girls would start with a brunch which lasted until the guys joined in for supper and then into an evening of dancing. We danced a lot back then.

Paul played racquetball for quite a while, but he was drawn to handball and over the years became competitive on a national level. He had the opportunity to travel to different tournaments across Canada. Brian would often show up to cheer him on.

Suzanne became a close friend. She was in an abusive relationship. Paul and I played a pivotal role in helping her disentangle. She and her daughter lived with us for 3 months in the transition.

A few years after us, Paul's sister Marilyn married. It was decided that they would add an addition to Paul's family home where she and their mom and dad still lived. Paul (now next door) helped, taking on more than his share. A finished product eventually came together. It was great that Marnie was there for her mom and dad.

Eventually, Paul's dad asked him to find a nursing home. Milton was a proud man and didn't want his children to be responsible for their care. We were able to secure them a room to themselves at Northwood Manor which was a new senior's care facility in Halifax. They were happy there for many years. Shannon got to visit as often as possible. He was a wonderful dog. He was a part of the family for about 14 years.

Life was full. We often shake our head over some of the things that we took on in addition to the work on our own property. The renovations we helped friends achieve, the furniture Paul built for them, the relationships that we supported over humps in their road.

It wasn't all work.

We hosted three huge summer parties bringing together all the people from the various groups we were part of - workmates, Y people, golf people, hunting and fishing buddies, hikers, etc. The numbers were well over 100 each time.

We had friends in the music business so they would set up and play for us. The fun would start mid-afternoon and it was not uncommon to feed 15 for breakfast. Lots of wood disappeared in those bonfires.

In the meantime, my jobs were changing. I left the secretarial position and for a time helped to market a new senior's complex. I had my first and last TV appearance, promoting the project on regional cable.

I eventually took an admin position with the provincial government in the Marketing and Trade Division. This took me to trade shows in Toronto and Montreal. I had never been on a plane so, prior to my first business trip, Paul and I flew to Prince Edward Island for the weekend.

Told you he is a romantic guy!

Politics can drive you crazy. That's one of the reasons Paul and I are a bit hawkish about who we vote for.

For example. I was invited to apply for a job in the Minister's office. I currently worked under a Director which was lower on the totem pole in the Department. It was apparent that even though I was recommended for the transfer, I was only a number on the Director's roster. My promotion to a better position outside his division would bring his numbers below a quota, so my job advancement was nixed. I was pissed.

That happened in the morning. I grabbed the newspaper, circled a few ads, made a phone call and went to an interview at noon. By 2 p.m. I tendered my resignation.

Yeah, in my tantrum, I didn't give much consideration to pensions and longevity. Ooops. That might have been a mistake, but that's life.

The job I went to was working with a prominent orthodontist with a staff of 9. I was familiar with how this treatment could change lives. It had done wonders for me, so I was happy working in this environment. I stayed about 10 years.

For the most part, it was a wonderful experience. I travelled to New York, Toronto and San Francisco. It paid well and I was encouraged to take on things outside of the admin duties like consultations with parents to explain treatment programs.

A parent of one of our patients was creating the Barrington Business Centre. I was invited to run it. That would be my next work adventure.

CHAPTER 15

Home
An Ugly Duckling
to Swan Story

In the 80s, we were starting to tackle some of the major projects on the property.

The interior of the house was comfortable enough at this point.

We had insulated the downstairs from the inside and added butterfly pine to the walls. All the windows were improved. The kitchen was redesigned and rebuilt with cedar cupboards. Everything in the house has our fingerprints.

Thank God Paul has carpentry skills, can wire a plug, install a floor. He is an all-around handy guy.

It was time to go outside.

The first thing to tackle was the sea wall. We had considered using concrete, but it was out of our budget. The cheapest and most attractive way would be to use rock.

We started by moving every rock of size we could from the beach and moving it into position about 4' out from the existing wood wall. When we ran out, trucks would deliver three different sizes of rock - boulders, 4" chunks and then gravel. It was hard to get the car close to the house at times.

Paul rigged up a plywood sleigh. Under that we used ABS rollers. The pattern was to use a crowbar to get the rock on the sleigh and then Paul would pull, and I would move the rollers down to where we could, ever so carefully, dump the rock over the wall and move it to where it would stay. Repeat this a few hundred times, back fill by hand with the 4" stone and cover with gravel. One layer at a time. It took us 3 years.

The average height of the wall is 7', 4' wide at the base tapered to 2' at the top. Our gift to ourselves when it was finished was a concrete top that we had poured. Paul estimates it took 450 tons of material.

Impressive accomplishment alongside the first rock wall (now on the neighbour's property) which he had built when his dad was alive.

My mom and dad would come from their home in Sackville (yes, they moved again!) every weekend to watch our progress on the wall. As did most boaters on Prospect Bay. We were a bit of a scratch-your-head spectacle. "These people are nuts."

Mom passed away in 1984 before the concrete was poured on the wall. She was the first of our four parents to die within a 7-year span. We also lost brother Bruce to cancer.

Our friends were having baby showers and we were planning funerals.

This circumstance, along with our care of elderly parents during our early married life, is a good part of why we did not have children. We had been parents to our parents. Every year we would have "the talk" and by the time I was in my mid 30s, we had discerned, through prayer, that having a child was not something God was calling us to do. We have no regrets. God seems to agree as we have lived a very blessed life.

The next project was building a retaining wall between us and our neighbour to the south. Total length was about 40'. The wall is lovely even today. Mortared stone with a concrete cap. That's what you see. What you don't see is the 3 ft. trench filled with steel reinforced cement.

The area between the house and the new retaining wall came into shape with the building of a ground level deck roughly 20' X 20' with an elevated deck on one quarter to reach the door. The icing on the cake was a 6' privacy fence to enclose the area.

I will share a few more of the larger projects Paul and I tackled and then fill in the gaps of what life looked like in our "spare" time.

We added the dining room and expanded the living room. Essentially the whole house toward the water. We layed 400 railway ties to build raised gardens between us and Prospect Road. Brian made the mistake of arriving for vacation just as the ties were ready to be filled with soil. ☺ We also created the pond, paths and planting areas.

A few years later

After reading this list of our projects, you are probably sharing the sentiment of the boaters who thought we had lost our minds. Yes, it was a lot of work, but we made it fun.

Paul and I had jobs. We were never career people trying to climb an invisible ladder to gain the attention or the status someone else gave it. We did not earn big salaries and often would joke that money was something *someone else* wanted. Unfortunately. Like banks, stores…! We would have loved a barter system.

We enjoyed working together. We took great satisfaction in accomplishing a good day's efforts, regardless of whether it required a hammer or a shovel. There were lots of beer breaks, time to swim or enjoy the sun.

Attitude is the key. We never labelled the time we spent as Work.

We thrived on equity. As the house improved, we would borrow against it for the next project. It was a sound investment.

CHAPTER 16

Balance is Important

We always tried to balance things out. Juxta positions would be an evening at Neptune Theatre, a movie, going to a game or simply a fancy dinner out. We still had lots of friends, we travelled a bit and enjoyed life.

Oh yeah, we raised the roof on a vintage Dodge van, fixed up the inside with comfy seats and bed, fridge, stove, "pottie" and lots of storage. It was our "hotel" when we visited friends for a few drinks or my sister who had moved with her husband and two sons to PEI. (What are the odds? She married a Paul too.) The van's crescendo was a trip to Florida with friends who had a similar vehicle.

When Paul started work with the Province of Nova Scotia, one of his colleagues introduced us to Amway. For those who don't recall, this was a home business opportunity selling primarily soap products. Their catalogue was constantly expanding, but that was the base.

We were attracted to the process more than the business. What we liked was the positive attitudes they promoted. The whole energy of it was exciting. There were rallies locally and in the States. It was a blast meeting people who shared your "anything is possible" outlook.

The biggest event was in the Carolina's where we also spent a day at the biggest fairground we could have imagined. It was not a long stay in the Amway world, but we gained a lot of insights into people. The experience was one that helped us mature.

This *be-a-better-person* kick, led us into more self-help areas. We started buying self-improvement books, such as "If You Don't Know Where You Are Going, You Will Probably End Up Somewhere Else". We listened to speakers such as Ekhart Tolle. You get the picture.

We didn't change our faith in God, but we were very taken with hearing other angles to the questions we always enjoyed exploring. Why are we here? What makes us tick?

One of our "finds" was an article entitled "Success versus Successful Living". It made sense to us. With this visual in mind, we were able to look at our lifestyle with a discerning eye and make some adjustments.

It became a tool that we would bring out every so often to help us **keep the joy in life greater than the stress.**

We will share the concept and hope that it will help in your life journey. Picture a circle divided into six equal slices, like a pie. Label each section with one of the major factors that affect every life. Social, Physical, Family, Financial, Mental, Spiritual. The goal is to keep these segments equal. That is virtually impossible. The exercise is to examine how you spend your time and evaluate if it is working for you. Is one section taking all your focus? The question to ask yourself, Is this Success or Successful Living?

Our own preference was to lean toward successful living.

Here are a few scenarios that we observed:

We knew people who worked hard to gain positions of influence in their field. We thought them to be workaholics. They had wealth and prestige. But, most often, they seemed to have stolen time from family and friends, their health appeared to be suffering and we did not see a spiritual component.

Lots of our friends devoted everything to their family. This was not necessarily a bad thing, but we witnessed people take it to extremes. Their children's schedules ruled the house, even to the point of missing church. They stopped taking time with and for each other.

Even community and church focused people we knew seemed to be out of balance. How could they spend that much time away from kids and their spouse?

<u>The important thing is to be aware</u>. Don't get caught up in putting one foot in front of the other and never stop to ask yourself if you are happy with the direction or the result. For us, at the time, we were spending too much time with the mental exploration, physical was time consuming, and parents took a big chunk. The other three suffered. The result was that we purposefully refocused and tried to level them off. Our spiritual journey was acknowledged as important, we often prayed and were thankful, but otherwise it was still the smallest piece of the pie.

Success vs. Successful Living was timely for us. We had been married about 20 years. Most of the people in our lives were in crisis. Marriages were falling apart. If they didn'tdivorce, they lived separate lives, each doing the things they liked but very little together.

Applying the pie concept, it was a fairly easy way for us topick up on the perceived imbalances in each situation and understand the cost they were paying for letting life get out of balance.

God is patient. He let us explore for a while before He called us back. But it wasn't time yet.

CHAPTER 17

Lessons in Appreciation

In 1989, we embarked on a great adventure.

Brian and Paul were finally getting their trip overseas but this one included me. After 16 years, Brian and I had gained an appreciation for each other and the three of us got along well. Brian had been to Greece a few times and loved it. So, like any good friend would, he wanted us to share in the experience.

We met up with him at Heathrow Airport. The next four weeks were wonderful. We explored Athens, Mykonos, Santorini, Crete, Rhodes, and Chios in Greece. Crossing to Turkey, we travelled south to Izmir to meet up with Turkish friends we had met in Halifax.

While we were away and sister, Marilyn, was in hospital, her husband dropped the bomb that he was leaving (with all the assets he could steal) and she was on her own. Nice timing if you are a prick. It didn't take long before it was evident that she would not be able to afford to stay in her house.

Just to add a bit of clarity, Marilyn and her husband had built an addition to her parent's home when they first married. However, when Milton and Muriel moved to Northwood, they sold and moved within walking distance to White's Lake, just at the head of the Bay.

Even though Marilyn had exclusively brought all the equity into the marriage, there was next to none left in the house as it had been used to finance the prick's business, which was deemed to be his and not common property. So, the home that Milton and Muriel worked hard to create on Prospect Bay, that was intended to be left to Paul and Marilyn, ended up benefitting the one person that contributed nothing. Life is not fair.

Marilyn came to live with us for the year it took us to build her home which would be self-contained but attached to us.

This required a God intervention because we did not have enough property.

Ethel was our neighbour on that side back then. She was Aunt Margaret's daughter, so a cousin to Paul and Marilyn. She generously gave us enough property to accommodate the build.

We will be forever grateful.

CHAPTER 18

The 90's

We lost my dad in 1991. He was the last parent to go. I was orphaned at 39 years old. Before that in fact. After mom died in 1984, dad was distant. He stopped visiting regularly and found excuses not to spend holidays together. I was hurt but obviously he was content to be a single, carefree guy for his last years.

In the next chunk of life, we were up to our eyeballs in building the addition for Marnie.

I won't bore you with the ups and downs. There were many. With very little money, we manually poured the foundation because the design had angles other than 90 degrees. No contractor would do the work.

It would take 18-hour days and many, many months of hard labour to get a completed house. We would get up early to be at the YMCA for exercise by 7 a.m. Paul and I would get home about 5:30 p.m. and work on the addition until dark, fall into bed and do it again the next day. You either get closer or you break. We got closer.

We used the fill created from digging the foundation to level the garage area. We also simultaneously built a garden house, two large sheds and started the 100 plus foot fence along the northern property line.

Paul and I were exhausted.

We had racked up enough travel points with the construction costs, so we treated ourselves to a trip once Marnie was settled in. We went to San Diego (first class which was an added bonus) for a few weeks to stay with a friend we had met while he was on a work assignment in Halifax. Mike and his family were gracious hosts. We thoroughly enjoyed seeing that part of the world.

Just to mix it up, when the 1992 national handball tournament came to Halifax, a handful of our players and their spouses hosted an extremely successful event. In addition to daily lunches, we provided a lobster supper at the banquet. Paul was on the phone to his cousin who delivered a fresh catch to us just in time to cook and serve.

It was a repeat performance. Nova Scotia Handball hosted a welcome booth at the Vancouver event the previous year. We served lobster rolls with Schooner beer. An homage to the Maritimes. To pull this off, Paul managed the cookers in gale force winds and our kitchen was full of people cleaning the lobster. It was worth the effort.

Work for me was now running a business centre. Umur, our Turkish friend, was a client. At his coaxing, Paul and I were encouraged to fulfil our original plan to revisit that part of the world.

In September 1992, we took a month off to travel back across the pond. This time, we would focus a bit more on Turkey, but also explore Greece again.

From London, we flew to Istanbul to stay with our first Turkish host, Veysi, Umur's best bud. While Veysi was at work, we found our way around but nothing beyond Paul's sense of direction helped. Signs were beyond our ability to decipher. We managed with help from the locals. The Blue Mosque was interesting. The Grand Bazaar was overwhelming.

We travelled by bus to Ankara where we met up with Umur and his girlfriend. Driving through the country opened our eyes to a very different way of life. Our Turkish friends were both considered affluent in their culture. They each had a comfortable residence, but most did not.

The country is quite beautiful. It produces every type of crop you can imagine. On the downside, the highways are non-stop diesel trucks transporting food to the city centres. If you drive with a window open, you are very quickly covered in black soot. They didn't lean toward catalytic converters back in the day. The air of oppression was also evident. We were privileged to have Turkish guides. We would not have relaxed otherwise. We were in a Muslim country, and it was a heavy environment. People generally did not smile or laugh in public and simple conversation often sounded sharp.

But with that said, we had a wonderful time. Our hosts were very kind to give us a memorable trip. One highlight was visiting Ephesus, a biblical landmark. It was thoughtful and meaningful for us to also see where our mother Mary spent her last days on earth. It was heart-warming to learn that the Muslim culture holds Mary in high esteem.

The drive from Ankara to the coast is quite long. It was a welcome change to be seaside again. We enjoyed Kusadasi. Great beaches. Further along the coast was Bodrum. We celebrated Paul's 45th birthday there with a fun boat ride and a great meal on the boardwalk.

Leaving Turkey from Marmaris, our mode of transportation was by hydrofoil. That was a unique boating thrill that took us back to Rhodes. We were very glad to be back in a Christian majority country. Yes. It makes a huge difference.

We were on our own now. No hosts and no Brian to help us find our way around. It was an exercise in trusting our own instincts. Nothing was prebooked except our flight from Athens back to Istanbul.

Everything in between was spontaneous. After a few days on Rhodes (where we literally stayed with a Greek family who took us under their wing), we decided to fly to Mykonos. That island was dear to us from our first trip, and it was great to see it again. Later in the week, we took a ferry to Piraeus.

We did have one target if time allowed. Friends from home were getting married in Greece. As it worked out, we were able to find them in Volos, north of Athens, to help them celebrate the occasion. It was providential (another way of saying it was a "God thing"), that we showed up.

There had been misunderstandings in their long-distance wedding arrangements which could have changed the mood. We were happy to witness for them. The summer dress I had just picked up in Rhodes came in handy and was the perfect match to the bride's colour scheme. Paul had a clean new shirt in his backpack too. God is good.

We made bus connections to Athens by the skin of our teeth to catch our flight back to Istanbul. Our last day in Turkey was perfect. Great weather, site seeing and a memorable feast with friends.

London was a place we had touched on during our first visit. This time, we took a bit of extra time to look around and take in a live theatre production of Miss Saigon. Great fish and chips! The whole menu was nothing but different types of fish and potatoes!

Vacations are fun but it was time to go home. We were looking forward to Prospect Bay.

CHAPTER 19

Rita at Work

Work changed for me a few more times. From the Business Centre, I went with a client who was starting a company that would recruit professionals to fill management positions. A headhunter. That took me down unexpected roads where I learned to interview and put discernment skills to use. After a few years, it was evident that I did not have the entrepreneurial drive to help build that business so back to admin for me.

I went to work for the VP of a privately owned development firm. Some of their properties would be familiar to anyone in Halifax. For example, they developed Historic Properties / Privateers Wharf and Founders Square to name a few. It was fun and they were a good company to their employees.

Then something funny happened. I was headhunted. Yup. What goes around, comes around. I would finish off the decade working for the President of a prominent architectural firm.

Paul was hanging in there (for my sake) at the Province of Nova Scotia. He was the one with a pension. He hated the politics of his job as much as I had, but he stuck it out long enough to get his long term service award and early retirement at age 55!

There were upsides though. He met a lot of nice people. Paul was easy going and knowledgeable so he was asked to mentor many of the professionals that springboarded through the department.

Because he didn't have a degree, personal upward momentum was limited, but the wealth of experience he brought to the job was immeasurable. One of the summer students that he directed was an out of province student, Helen, who was destined for a career in HR / Statistics following her Masters.

The next February (1996), she called to invite us to join her, a couple of girlfriends and her dad on a sailing trip in the British Virgins. (We thought it was a joke because we had just booked a weekend at a local resort that was offering a Caribbean themed winter getaway). It wasn't a joke. Her dad wanted another male on board to share the responsibilities and she immediately thought of Paul.

A few weeks later we boarded a beautiful 34' sloop named Magic. Helen's dad had taken the boat from its home port in New England to the Caribbean. His "pay" was his personal use of the boat for a month. We got to enjoy the experience for 10 days!! We sailed from Sint Maarten to St. Thomas, through the Sir Francis Drake Channel to Puerto Rico. It is in the top 5 of our travels for sure.

CHAPTER 20

Brian, Part Two

After decades of going back and forth, Brian retired from his position and moved east. Yes, he moved in with us.

I came home from work one day and my living room furniture was gone. Brian's was in its place along with a ton of brass and wicker. Paul wanted to make sure he felt at home. So, out with some of our stuff to make room for Brian's. That was just the surface stuff. Brian needed family, not a roof over his head. He had been battling alcoholism all his adult life.

A bit of history…Given that our time together over the decades of friendship was sporadic, our reunions were always a party and so Brian's problem with booze did not come to light for a long time. Paul came to this realization during one of his visits and spoke to Brian about seeking help. He tried.

The years of AA meetings began with us cheerleading from afar. It wasn't enough. The problem was progressive. Brian was not doing his best at work and this was putting his position in jeopardy. He had been a hardworking, effective director, often with hundreds of people in his department. His employer offered an attractive early retirement package which Brian accepted.

That's when Paul and I made the decision to expand our family once again and Brian came into the household.

It was the right thing to do. It wasn't easy. There were many rough roads ahead for all of us. Brian was still in addiction.

A blended family, regardless of ages, is difficult. Paul and I were not alone in making adjustments and learning the skills that would make our expanded family a happy one. But, with God's help, the four of us (Paul, me, Brian and Marilyn) each contributed to building a loving home. At the time of writing, 20+ years in, we are still a family... all of us are older and closer to the inevitable, but it has been a blessing all around.

Talk about blessings!! After a decades long struggle, Brian has achieved sobriety through an understanding of God's love for him.

With all our faults and flaws, God was guiding each of us to help others.

Some call this "ministry".

CHAPTER 21

Ministry
What does that have to do with us?

Ministry conjures up an image of something formal, probably with a religious connotation. It was a scary word for us. Time and a bit of wisdom has taught us differently.

For example, Brian started by simply helping others achieve sobriety. It was part of his own recovery. Over time (years), one God nudge after another, he finally landed on the 12 Steps with Christ program.

Without calling it by name, he had a "ministry" !!

Paul and I had not gone to church for years. We did not intend to go to church in the foreseeable future. Remember I told you that God does things in his own time. He had never let go of our hands and it had always been a comfort to know He was there, even though we didn't talk as often as we should have. Our choice, not His.

Life was about to deliver a gut punch. God knew that the early 2000 years would bring many heartaches, so He made sure we reunited with our faith to help us through the tough times that lay ahead.

Hindsight tells us that. We didn't know what we were about to experience. God knew that being part of helping others (ministry of sorts) would, in fact, help us.

It all started with a funeral. Friends had lost their parents in a very short period which took us to the neighbourhood Catholic church for both services.

We were new faces, so the priest approached us and was surprised at our response to his question. "Who are you?" Are you ever shocked at what comes out of your own mouth? We said, we are parishioners! What we meant was, we live in the area.

Not one to miss an opportunity, Fr. Derek was sitting at our dining table within the week. My arms firmly crossed over my chest didn't seem to slow him down much. I should have remembered this posture wouldn't work on a priest. ☺

Paul was the first to succumb to his charm. He agreed to attend a one-day men's retreat at the parish that Saturday. Sarcastically. I thought "great".

Of course, Paul had a wonderful day. He met some great guys and he came home really committed to renewing his attention to faith and prayer. He wanted to go back to weekly Mass AND he started saying The Rosary every day. Mass I agreed with. The little voice in my head was saying it was time, but the Rosary, that was out of my comfort zone.

It was odd for us not to do things together. I knew Paul was praying the Rosary when I was out, and it bugged me. I guess

a better word would be, it "convicted" me. Okay, Okay…
I'll try it. At first, the prayer seemed ridiculous to me. Too
repetitive. I didn't know it was supposed to be a meditation
on the life of Jesus.

Like exercising any muscle, the more you try, the better it
gets. Together, over time, Paul and I fell in love with the
Rosary. It is truly a wonderful gift and a powerful weapon
against evil. We pray together every day.

We were back in the pews. It didn't take Fr. Derek long to stir
up an enthusiasm in the parish for evangelization. Unlike our
previous church experience, Fr. was a let'smake something
happen, leader. The tool he chose was The Saint Andrew
School of Evangelization.

There are dozens of themes in the school, all designed to grow
your relationship with our Lord. "*School*" sounds boring,
but it was anything but. Full of activities, discussions, fun,
music … all painlessly taking you on a journey of faith.

We learned much and matured more in this environment.

About 20 people made up the teams and we often travelled
to Ontario and Quebec to meet and learn from other SASE
communities. It took a lot of our time and focus. We were
very glad to be back in Christian community. It was what
saved us from despair.

Sorry for the build-up, but you need some background going
back a few years.

From the architectural firm, I was lured to a job that seemed too good to be true. The offer was a 4-day work week (down from 5) at the same salary. I was thrilled to reunite with a client I had worked with at the Business Centre.

Glenn operated a small business which offered equipment leasing finance solutions to a variety of business needs. The money was funded from various sources, usually banks, insurance companies, etc. We simply found the opportunities and brokered the arrangements on a commission.

A few years into this work environment, it was Glenn's observation that a private investment group could also be used as a funding source. It was a sound idea. Interested parties reviewed the rationale and groups formed across the country. It worked well, until it didn't.

No one really knows how it went sour, but, the result, was that the funds were manipulated so that people were being defrauded. I still believe that Glenn had honourable intentions but somewhere a line was crossed which resulted in people losing a lot of money. Glenn was suddenly dodging angry phone calls.

It was obvious that something was not right. Glenn was evasive and noncommunicable. As a solution to separation from whatever he had gotten into, my good friend and colleague Rhonda and I started a separate company. For Glenn's sake, we marketed it as a "branch". We went back to industry leasing standards leaving Glenn with the "investment" business.

Rhonda and I had zero income for a long time but at least we had a window of opportunity to build one. Glenn was on his own and we hoped that he would be able to right the ship. We both loved Glenn as a friend and thought we knew that his heart was in the right place.

This is the tragedy that was awaiting us.

Glenn solved the problem by taking his own life.

It was devastating. The rumours were horrible.

Paul and I lost our savings and, on top of that, we had borrowed to invest in Glenn's business. As it was structured as a term investment, we couldn't draw it out when I left work.

We had to scramble to make ends meet. With my salary gone and Paul retired (since 2002), the bills were mounting. We sold everything that was available to sell leaving only the house and one car.

It was very hard to keep a positive attitude. Life was a roller coaster of faith highs and money lows.

After Glenn's death, we learned that he had left a life insurance policy with me as the beneficiary. I had always kidded him about my vulnerability should he be "hit by a bus". I had no idea he had taken it seriously.

The amount pretty much equalled our debt. We were elated. Then the estate assets were challenged by the many debtors and the policy was confiscated. Paul and I sought legal assistance and a prominent firm offered to take on the case for 30% of the value. We agreed.

There was a time that we thought we would lose the house. That was another pivotal point in our life.

A year went by. We were surviving, barely. We answered a phone call and were given the news that the lawyers had dropped their efforts on our petition to recover the insurance money.

If you have ever felt the wind being forced out of your lungs, it was like that. We were gasping for air. Despair is a dark place. You can't see your way out. Hope is elusive and faith is shaken.

Paul and I went to open water. Literally. We got in a boat and went to a remote part outside of the bay. Despair has a distinctive sound. At the top of his lungs, Paul called out to God. What I am about to share is our miracle. It did not give us solutions or change the problems we faced. It simply brought us peace.

As soon as Paul cried out to God, a bird soared over the boat. It was about the size of a large eagle, but it was pure white. Not from here. For about 40 minutes, it circled and dove in the water all around us. This was not normal. The sun made the bird appear to glow. We knew it was God's way to tell us that we were not alone. It gave us hope.

Earlier we told you that God had made sure that we would have a Christian community around us in tough times. That very day, we were heading to our first SASE gathering. We took our eyes off the bird long enough to start the motor. In that instant, it was gone. We could see for miles in all directions. It was simply gone.

Diversion is a good temporary cure. We went to the meeting and started on a wonderful, almost decade-long journey that would help us better understand the things that were important in our life.

God and each other: that about summed it up.

Months later we said *out loud* to God in prayer that if we had to choose between losing everything we owned or losing our faith, we would choose our faith. It was and is our anchor.

It was also a turning point.

The lawyer who had abandoned us 8 months earlier called!! He asked if I could be in court the following week. I assumed it had to do with the salary that had been unpaid prior to my leaving Glenn's employ. There is a pecking order when money from a contested estate is paid out. Employee wages are among the priorities.

So, I went to court and was shocked to learn that our lawyer was arguing that I was the legal beneficiary under the policy Glenn had set aside for me. What? Why? The answer was born of the lawyer's pride, but it changed our life.

The lawyer told me that much earlier in the negotiations with the bankruptcy insolvency advocate, he had suggested that they "throw me a bone" and they had refused. He didn't like their attitude and somewhere, somehow, it was **now** in his head to challenge them.

Thankyou Holy Spirit!

Our lawyer made a concise presentation pointing to the timelines involved which would exclude the policy from the business assets in dispute. The opposing counsel was late, ruffled, ill prepared and overall ignorant and overbearing. He grilled me on the stand in unpleasant tones and innuendo.

Four days later, we picked up a cheque for the full amount of the policy minus the 30% commission which we paid glady.

There is no question in our minds that God heard our sincerity, and He rewarded our faithfulness.

After this dark patch, in 2009, Paul, Brian and I decided that we needed to do something fun together; so we embarked on another adventure.

The main event was Croatia mainland and islands but we travelled through Austria, Italy, Slovenia and Germany. Venice was a bucket list item.

CHAPTER 22

Life Goes On

Be grateful in all things.

Being back on a financial footing was a gift we have never taken for granted. We learned well from our foray into greed and material focus. With gratitude came a need to give back whenever we could.

As part of our "thank you" to God, in 2013, we joined a pilgrimage led by Fr. Derek. The journey would take us to Rome, Italy and Poland. The timing coincided with the canonization of Pope John Paul II.

Rome first. The day before the canonization, our guide managed to get us into St. Peter's Basilica even though it was closed to the public. Another "blessing". We spent hours touring the cathedral. We hadn't realized that there were many chapels within, each with their own altars, stations and focus for prayer. My personal favourite was the Pieta sculpture.

We were also treated to see parts of the Vatican Museum where we walked through vast hallways filled with art history. The cherry on top was a full 45 minutes in the Sistine chapel. Anyone familiar with the typical visit to this landmark will attest that it is unheard of to have that opportunity. The norm is to be shuttled through without stopping. That day, It was only our group of about 40 people. We could lie on the floor and stare at the ceiling or stroll around the room following the story being told in the paintings.

All in all, Rome was wonderful but, in full disclosure, we will never again choose to be in a million person plus crowd. It was overwhelming.

The day of the event was a very early start. Even at 4 a.m. we were blocks away from the Vatican and people were shoulder to shoulder both ahead of us and behind. Paul and I opted to return to the hotel.

The day before we covered the same ground in 20 minutes. Because of the traffic barricades, media trucks and the sheer volume of people, it took us a couple of hours for the return trip. That was nerve racking and very disorienting. Safely back in our hotel room, we were content to watch the service from the comfort of our bed.

By the afternoon, the crowds were gone, and the city was virtually empty. Paul and I took the opportunity to explore. We walked for miles around the old city, crisscrossing the sporadic bridges that span the Tiber. Looking down the banks of the river, hints of civilizations past are layered in a mosaic of patterns in the sediment. Our imaginations conjured up visions of all the saints who have walked those streets. It was a lovely day. The Trevi Fountain, of course, was a highlight.

Poland is a beautiful country. It is impossible to recall every town. The names are not easy for us English speaking folk. Here is a glimpse of the memories. Visiting Fr. Derek's home and meeting his mom and dad. We followed in the footsteps of Sister Faustina Kowalska. Visited the Divine Mercy Campus. Saw where Pope John Paul II spent a portion of his life. Our tour took us on a round trip passing through some of the larger cities like Warsaw and Krakow. We also visited Auschwitz and the salt mines. Both left indelible impressions.

Back home, SASE had started to conclude its season in our life. Our parish priest and SASE leader, Fr. Derek, was reassigned to a parish in Dartmouth. At first it seemed we would be able to keep offering SASE from his new location which had better course facilities.

However, the priorities of the incoming parish pastor were at odds with a core group of his congregation working outside of his "domain" even though evangelization is, by its nature, an outreach.

The parish focus would now be Alpha. The new priest asked Paul and I to attend an Alpha training course that was being offered at Saint Benedict parish in Halifax. Our mission was to learn how to bring this method back to our parish.

About 50 people from various parishes in the diocese sporadically filled the first five rows. The (since) legendary Fr. James Mallon was the speaker. He was halfway through a sentence when he stopped, looked directly at Paul, pointed and said his name. After a brief hesitation, he looked at me and then back at Paul and said: *"You gave the marriage talk on my retreat weekend."* OMG That would have been 30 years earlier!

Although we gave it a good try, the conflicts arising from a clash of egos in our home parish drove us to look for a new spiritual home. The new priest resented our closeness to his predecessor and constantly tried to berate us, SASE and all the good things that had come from it.

When the homily is designed to throw daggers and you often leave the church in tears, it isn't a huge leap to decide to leave a toxic environment. Before we acted on that decision, we reached out out for counselling. Fr. James graciously gave us an hour of his time. We found, or, more accurately, we were led by another God Nod to our new spiritual home... at Saint Benedict parish.

(In time it was understood the offensive priest suffered from Asperger Syndrome. He was reassigned out of parish leadership. It was comforting to know that the ugliness had no rationale.)

CHAPTER 23

Growing Relationship

Relationships mature. Even the one with yourself. It's odd to watch yourself get older. Only you know the changes that, although they are not always visible on the outside, you know they are life changing. Your values change, the way you view the world changes. Of course, you look different.

It requires a new level of maturity to age gracefully.

To understand that the physical things you took pride in earlier in life are being compensated for in other ways, is also a grace.

Paul and I are still in love. Does that look the same over the years? Fundamentally, the answer is Yes.

True love is eternal. It doesn't change. It just gets better, ripens, blooms. Given time and nurturing, all relationships will follow this growth path, including your relationship with your creator. It is central to peace of mind and wisdom.

Because Paul and I have always delved into "big issue" topics, and this type of conversation is normal for us, we have not lost each other on the journey.

Understanding that our relationship with God is the foundation that enables our marriage to continue to grow, we arrived at Saint Benedict parish ready to serve.

Compared to our Prospect Bay community parish, Saint Benedict was a bit imposing. It was physically 5 or 6 times larger. A typical Mass attendance went from 50 locally to 650! Quite a change.

In an effort to meet people, one of the first things we did was join a study group. The topic was "The Mass". As this thanksgiving celebration is the Source and Summit of our Catholic faith, we were keen to learn more. Yes, I know you think we are already saturated in all things Catholic, but there is always something to discover. It was a great course and we did learn a lot.

Paul joined a 7 a.m. Friday morning men's group which gave a platform for guys to share fellowship and bits of their faith journey. That gave rise to joining other groups and before long we were active participants in the parish. Service led us in directions we did not always consciously choose. We experienced Alpha, worked as team on future Alpha courses, joined a Connect Group, took over the lead on the Mass study, served on the altar, became Eurcharistic ministers, sponsored people who were preparing to become Catholic and eventually led that program for a few years.

Paul had an additional "ministry". His love language is gifts. He put his God given talent to work. He has made and distributed hundreds of pocket crosses. Stories have come back to us about how they comforted people at the hour of their death or helped them through serious illness and times of stress. He also made Tau crosses. Hundreds of them. Participants in a men's conference each went away with one around their neck.

Added to those gifts, he also made a multitude of stands so that people would be encouraged to have a bible openly displayed in their home. Marilyn helped by painting each one, twice! Although not handmade, he also distributed dozens of prayer rings. A little item to carry in your pocket as a reminder to pray. Paul has also donated 600 pints of blood. I am proud of him.

Being part of the "leadership team", two of hundreds in the parish who shared that calling, was exhilarating. If that has never been your church experience, we understand. Been there too. Don't lose heart. It can exist but it takes effort on everyone's part to grow the mission of spreading the joy of being Christian.

Paul and I have an added motivation. God gave us the last name "Christian" and an occasional kick in the bum, as a reminder to BE one. That is still a work in progress.

There are people along the way that "cross" your path. Pun intended. We have shared that Father James was a force of nature in influencing changes for the good within our faith community. That message eventually spread worldwide in the wake of his book *Divine Renovation*. The person who was able to apply these principles to change the culture of Saint Benedict was Ron Huntley.

Ron and James were friends from an early age. They shared the same vision for evangelizing the Catholic methodology. The church at large needed to do a better job to help people see the fullness and richness of Catholic traditions.

While Fr. James was unparalleled in arousing a full auditorium, Ron excelled in devising ways to bring their shared principles into practice. When Saint Benedict was a newly built church, Fr James was assigned to lead the parish. His first recruit was Ron.

Paul had become friends with Ron through the men's group. We both had interactions with him as he was the lead staff person, directing all things that influenced the culture at Saint Benedict.

The goal was to create a place where people felt valued, were encouraged to grow and share their faith. The parish was in full stride when Paul and I arrived. That's why it was so easy to find ways to serve. All we had to do was say "yes".

Fr. James and Ron were breaking new ground. They became sought after speakers in the Catholic world. Saint Benedict was on the map and people were watching. One day, I happened to be sitting next to Ron at Mass. He looked very tired. It was another one of those times when you don't expect the words to come out of your mouth. I heard myself offering my admin services.

I was still working with Rhonda, but my work arrangement was flexible. Ron and I worked together for about a year. He and Fr. James had created a new ministry, Divine Renovation, named for the original book. This teaching ministry was now busy enough to move out of the SBP basement to an actual office dedicated to the cause. Ron transitioned the SBP staff to be self-sustaining and focused his full-time attention to Divine Renovation.

A few years later, we would work together again. This time, Ron called to ask me to join him at Divine Renovation ministry, the SAME DAY Rhonda and I had decided to close our business. Holy Spirit at work again!

Six months later, Ron and I would leave DR to launch Huntley Leadership. I helped with admin services for the first year. Ron's ministry is a blessed venture with funds coming together as they are needed. It is thriving. Paul and I love seeing the Holy Spirit at work!

There is a season for all things. It was time for me to step away. The friendship, though, will be for a lifetime. It is one both Paul and I treasure.

CHAPTER 24

Another Gift

God has always had a hold of our hands. Paul and I often didn't realize it until time had passed and we could look back and relive the situations with a clearer perspective. Things that once seemed very hurtful, in time, were blessings in disguise.

We believe this happens to all of us.

Grace is being able to recognize those times when we are led by the Holy Spirit.

Earlier in this book, we described the lot that Muriel (née Duggan) and Milton bought from her sister Margaret. This is where Paul and I live today.

If you remember, the property was opposite a small island. It measures roughly one-half acre. The island coverage is a mixture of hard and soft wood varieties: birch, maple, spruce and fir. The shoreline is primarily granite. The elevations are just a few feet above sea level with one small hill. Not a lot to capture anyone's interest, but we will give you a bit of history that ties into our story.

Both of Paul's parents can trace their ancestry to the Duggan and Christian families that first settled Prospect and surrounding areas in the 1700's. Because there was no land registry process, the families were basically squatters for the first century.

The first legal grant of land at the head of Prospect Bay (including the island) and part of the shore on White's Lake, was awarded to Paul's ancestor, John Christian, in 1837. The land was traded, or sold, a few times over the next 50 years. In 1916, the owner was a great granddaughter of John Christian.

Over time, members of the Christian and Duggan families married. To condense the course of history, in 1949, remnants of those families, signed a deed for property at the head of Prospect Bay, which included the island, over to the Catholic Church. The use was to be a summer camp for children. That intention was never realized. The island was forgotten.

The island remained in the Church's possession until 2016 when Paul approached the Bishop. He was able to purchase the island in time to give it to me as a Christmas present. What a surprise!! A full circle of sorts. Just a hundred yards away from our home, this inclusion secured for us the privacy of owning land on both sides of our little piece of Prospect Bay.

We were shocked that it was even possible for it to be ours.

Welcome to PROSPECT BAY

Looking north, the island is **Christian Isle.**
White's Lake is in the distance.

Paul and I live opposite Christian Isle to the left

Eveleigh's Beach was the open land in the foreground surrounded by sand

The opposite aerial photo shows **Christian Isle.**

Our **Home** is the centre property with gravel boatyard, hardscape, lawn and long wharf

To the left is the land formerly owned by **Aunt Margaret.**

To the right, **Paul's boyhood home**

The **rock wall** we built spans from the boat yard, right, to the end of the curved shoreline including the solid portion of the wharf

The island was badly damaged. There were dozens of downed trees, eroded shorelines and it had been disrespected, evidenced by a ton of abandoned debris. It was in dire need of TLC.

Given our stewardship nature, we believe the island was entrusted to us knowing that we would do our best to salvage this little piece of paradise.

We saw it as a gift from God.

At the time of writing, we are still in that process. There is no shortage of dead trees to clear to make new growth possible. We have planted and pruned, built retaining walls, erected a small shed to hold the tools and raised a sign and flag.

Finally, after almost 200 years, the original pioneer family's name can be found on a map. As of May 27, 2021, the island proudly bears the name Christian Isle. John would be pleased.

It is a peaceful, contemplative place. Our hope is that its "christian" nature will be a legacy to anyone who visits.

Christian Isle as seen from our backyard

CHAPTER 25

A Straight Stretch
on the Journey

Coronavirus (COVID-19) SARS-CoV-2 entered the world's vocabulary in early 2020. At the time, Paul and I were still active at Saint Benedict parish surrounded by people who shared a common belief and faith in God.

Covid has also been a shared experience. Not only in our own parish but by people worldwide. It has been a time of confusion and uncertainty.

Like with all challenges, Paul and I talked through the possible controversies of this event and came to a common view which has been another blessing. Many families have not been so fortunate.

Regardless of the choices any of us have made with regard to Covid, no one has been spared the grief of seeing people sick or dying. It has been a heartbreak that we as human beings have suffered together.

Because Paul and I are people of faith, we trust that from this horrible chapter in everyone's journey, in time, there will be a collective healing. God will find a way to make lemonade from lemons.

We are finally able to congregate to celebrate Mass. It's funny how many things in life complete a full circle. Time has a way of doing that. So, a bit surprisingly, we decided to return to our community church and not to Saint Benedict. It was in our heart that, maybe, this was where we were supposed to be.

Part of prayer is trying to discern what message we are meant to hear. It's like when someone whispers in your ear but you are not really sure you heard correctly. It makes you lean in a bit closer and pay attention.

Discernment is difficult. Our journeys teach us to seek and find. Ask and receive.

Paul and I see this exercise through the eyes of faith but, we believe, <u>no matter where you are on your journey with God</u>, time spent in contemplation is very important.

God is always present and waiting for your invitation.

Psalm 46:10

"Be still and know that I am God."

CHAPTER 26

Today

Now (2023) in our 70's, Paul and I are in a season of gratitude. The busyness of life can be set aside at our choosing. There is time to reflect.

One of our greatest joys is that, looking back, there are very few things we would have done differently. That is a wonderful feeling.

We have matured and so has Prospect Bay.

This area was cottage country back in the 50s. The majority of properties on the Bay were seasonal even when Paul and I took up residence in 1977. Eveleigh's Beach no longer exists. Three elegant homes now occupy that land. The houses that line Prospect Bay, for the most part, are expensive. Many are valued well over $1,000,000.

Change is sometimes difficult.

Now, looking across the water from our home at night, we see lights on in various homes, (even streetlights!) where there was once wilderness. We were a bit selfish in our hesitancy to share the solitude and beauty of Prospect Bay but, on the flip side, it is truly heart-warming to see the happiness that being in nature brings to more and more families.

Hopefully Christian Isle will play a part.

Dozens of properties look at this little island every day. As time passes, softwoods, maples, willow and rose bushes we have planted or nurtured, will enhance their views and hopefully bring a smile to their face. Better still, instil a respect and gratitude for God's creation in their hearts.

That is our hope for Christian Isle.

Parting Thoughts

- We are all beloved, unique children of God.
- We all live a life that, in many ways, is solitary.
- That's why a **sacramental** marriage is a miracle.

Should that be **your** choice, you are offered the gift of navigating life with a third set of hands. God's. You never need to be without hope or help.

Because Paul and I did not follow the life path of parenting, we have a different legacy to offer. Simply our experience.

We have a loving, nurturing relationship. Our marriage is 50 years old and still vital.

Daily we say to each other "Have I told you today?" which is our code for I Love You. Every day we share stimulating conversation and an abundance of hugs and heartfelt kisses.

God willing, we will enjoy that sacrament for many years to come.

We wish the same for you.

Please remember:

Relationship IS something you grow.

We pray that some of our insights will help you grow the relationships in your journey.

Offered with love and encouragement:

Paul and Rita Christian